JUN 2 9 2007

In memory of Sky
and for the Homeyglomeys, with love
—P. E. N.

For Anna Marlis Burgard, the composer of this volume
—M. D. N.

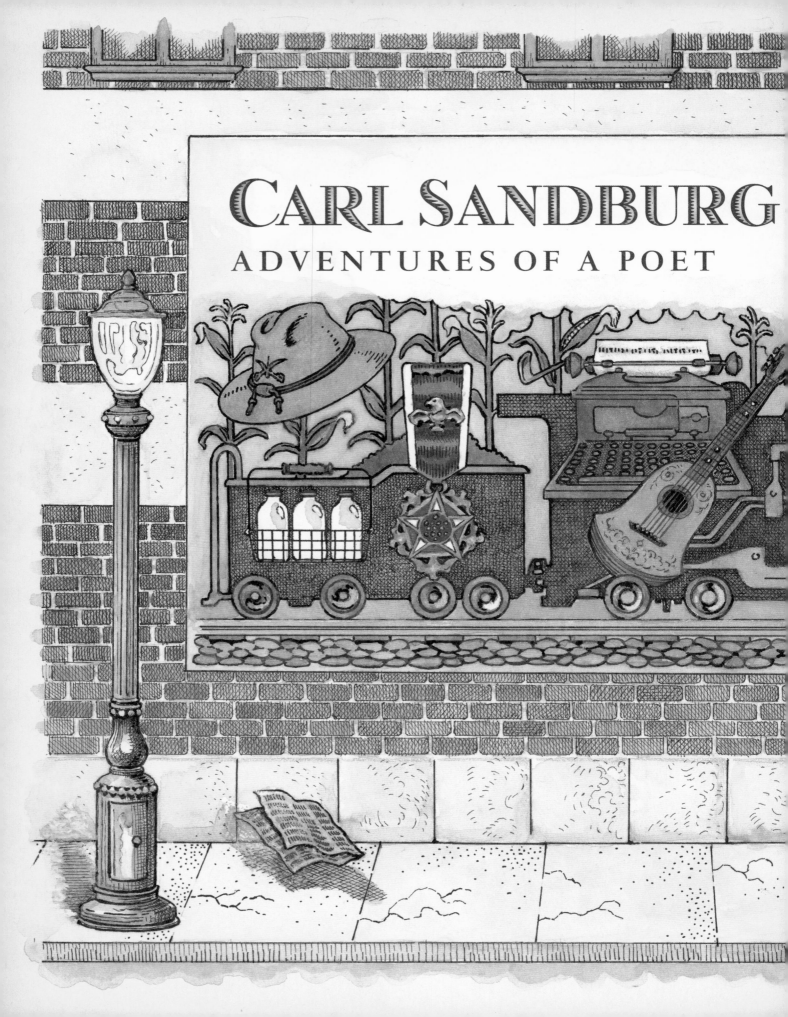

CARL SANDBURG

ADVENTURES OF A POET

PENELOPE NIVEN

With Poems and Prose by Carl Sandburg

ILLUSTRATED BY **MARC NADEL**

Harcourt, Inc.

Orlando • Austin • New York • San Diego • Toronto • London

Printed in Singapore

A WORLD OF WORDS

Carl August Sandburg was born on a corn-husk mattress in a three-room house in Galesburg, Illinois, soon after midnight on January 6, 1878. The first words drifting into his ears were *"Det är en pojke!"* Swedish for "It is a boy!" Carl was the first son of Clara and August Sandburg, who had left their homes in Sweden as young adults to start new lives in the United States.

Carl grew up loving words—the Swedish words his parents spoke at home and the English words he learned at school. As soon as he could read and write, he started collecting words in pocket notebooks. When he discovered a word that sounded good in his ears, felt good on his tongue, or puzzled his mind, he wrote it down. Just as children today collect stamps or baseball cards, Carl collected words. He wove them into poems and stories throughout his life.

As a shy boy from an immigrant family, Carl felt like an outsider in Galesburg. He wanted to be just like his friends—to talk like they did and dress like they did. When Carl spent time alone, watching trains come and go, he dreamed about traveling to faraway places.

Like many children who grow up to be writers, Carl explored the world through books. The first book he owned, *Cyclopaedia of Important Facts of the World,* was packed full of stories about history and heroes. Carl read almost every book in his school library—biographies, adventure stories, and poetry. Inspired by what he read, he began to write his own stories and poems.

When he went off to war as a young soldier, Carl sent stories home to the *Galesburg Evening Mail.* Later he wrote for the *Chicago Daily News* and other papers. He walked city streets, talking to people, learning about their problems, and reporting what he heard and saw. Because a journalist is trained to tell a big story in a small space, Carl learned to make every word count. Whether he was writing stories or poems, he paid careful attention to what the words meant and how they sounded.

Carl's first poem, "The Falling Leaves," was published in 1902. In 1914, after years of hard work, he won his first poetry prize for the poem "Chicago"—two hundred dollars, a sum that he said "octupled" his bank account. Carl's first successful book, *Chicago Poems*, was published in 1916, when he was thirty-eight. *Honey and Salt*, his last book, was published in 1963, when he was eighty-five. As a poet, historian, and storyteller, he wrote more than forty books in all.

Carl's best-known poem is "Fog," which was published in *Chicago Poems*. He wrote it after he walked along the Lake Michigan shore one day and saw fog covering the Chicago harbor:

> The fog comes
> on little cat feet.
>
> It sits looking
> over harbor and city
> on silent haunches
> and then moves on.

By the time Carl was a grandfather, so many people had asked him to recite "Fog" that he had fun changing the famous words: "The fog comes on itti bitti kitti footsies. / He sits down on Chicago and—whamo—he's gone."

Carl was called the Poet of the People because his poems speak to children, parents, farmers, city workers, homemakers, politicians, and many other people, not only in the United States but also around the world. The words Carl Sandburg wrote made him one of the most famous Americans of the twentieth century.

A NEW AMERICAN

Carl, his three sisters, and three brothers were new Americans—the first people in their family to be born in the United States. Carl's parents had traveled thousands of miles from their homes in Sweden to find work. Clara and August Sandburg believed that if they and their children worked hard enough, they could make their American Dream come true.

Twenty thousand people lived in Carl's hometown, and almost seventeen hundred of them worked for the railroad, including Carl's father, a blacksmith's helper. Day and night, trains clattered and whistled through Galesburg. When the circus train rumbled into town, Carl ran to the station to watch as clowns, acrobats, and elephants marched off and paraded down Main Street. To earn a free ticket to the circus, he carried water for the elephants.

Carl left school when he was thirteen to help earn money for his family. He worked ten-hour days delivering newspapers and doing odd jobs, making about twelve dollars a month. When he was fourteen, he worked as a "milk slinger," delivering milk for a dairy. Seven days a week, he walked two miles through the countryside to work. During those long walks, he watched prairie farmers plow and then plant their fields with wheat or Indian corn. He saw red clover growing by zigzag rail fences. On hot summer days, he walked dusty country roads. On icy winter days, he trudged along the gravel bed of the railroad tracks. Carl's feet nearly froze because there wasn't enough money to buy warm boots. He was always glad when spring came.

JUST BEFORE APRIL CAME

The snow-piles in dark places are gone.
Pools by the railroad tracks shine clear.
The gravel of all shallow places shines.
A white pigeon reels and somersaults.

Frogs plutter and squidge—and frogs beat
      the air with a recurring thin
      steel sliver of melody.
Crows go in fives and tens; they march their
      black feathers past a blue pool; they
      celebrate an old festival.
A spider is trying his webs, a pink bug sits
      on my hand washing his forelegs.
I might ask: Who are these people?

VAGABOND

In June 1897, when he was nineteen and hungry for adventure, Carl rode the train west to Kansas. Instead of packing a suitcase, he filled his pockets with soap, a razor, a comb, a pocket mirror, two handkerchiefs, a watch, a knife, and a pipe and tobacco. In one pocket he hid all his money—three dollars and twenty-five cents.

Except for going to Chicago and to Peoria for the Illinois State Fair, Carl had never traveled far from Galesburg. Now he was a vagabond, a person who wanders from place to place. Like other vagabonds who didn't have money for train tickets, Carl jumped aboard freight trains and hid in boxcars or on top of a train's caboose. One cold, starry night, he hopped a freight train in Colorado. He rode outside, between two boxcars, clinging to the brake rods. While the train chugged up the steep Rocky Mountains, Carl held on tight. Sometimes vagabonds fell under a moving train and were crippled or even crushed to death. Carl knew the danger, but he was so tired he could not stay awake. He pummeled his head with his fists and kicked one leg against the other, yet still he fell asleep. Just in time, the train jolted to a stop and woke him up. Carl was thankful to be alive.

To earn money Carl worked on the railroad in Missouri, harvested wheat in Kansas, and chopped wood in Nebraska. By September he was tired and homesick. With fifteen dollars and a few nickels in his pocket, Carl headed home. But he would always love to travel, free as a leaf in the wind.

BABY SONG
OF THE FOUR WINDS

Let me be your baby, south wind.
Rock me, let me rock, rock me now.
Rock me low, rock me warm.
Let me be your baby.

Comb my hair, west wind.
Comb me with a cowlick.
Or let me go with a pompadour.
Come on, west wind, make me your baby.

North wind, shake me where I'm foolish.
Shake me loose and change my ways.
Cool my ears with a blue sea wind.
I'm your baby, make me behave.

And you, east wind, what can I ask?
A fog comfort? A fog to tuck me in?
Fix me so and let me sleep.
I'm your baby—and I always was.

SOLDIER

Carl was working as a housepainter when he heard that the United States would go to war to help Cuba and Puerto Rico win their freedom from Spain. President William McKinley declared war on April 25, 1898, and the next day, Carl joined Company C, Sixth Infantry Regiment, Illinois Volunteers. He was now a soldier.

In an army camp near Washington, D.C., Carl learned to march and to fire his rifle. In his free time he visited the Capitol, the White House, and Ford's Theatre, where President Abraham Lincoln had been shot in 1865, just thirteen years before Carl was born.

In July 1898 Company C traveled by ship to Puerto Rico. Carl reported in the *Galesburg Evening Mail* about how he and his fellow soldiers waded ashore in deep water, dressed in hot wool uniforms left over from the Civil War and holding their rifles over their heads. They saw their first palm and coconut trees. Swarms of mosquitoes bit the soldiers until the men's eyes were swollen shut. The soldiers marched for eight miles through the mountains, where they heard shots in the dark and saw white puffs of smoke from gunfire.

The war ended in August, and on September 21, thousands of Galesburg citizens gathered at the train station to welcome Carl and the men of Company C home as heroes. Twenty years later, in 1918, Carl traveled to Sweden to write newspaper stories about soldiers and battles in World War I. Beginning in 1942 he wrote about World War II for newspapers throughout the United States. He also wrote poems describing the scenes and sounds of wartime, and the battlefields that stand empty and quiet after wars end.

NEW FEET

Empty battlefields keep their phantoms.
Grass crawls over old gun wheels
And a nodding Canada thistle flings a purple
Into the summer's southwest wind,
Wrapping a root in the rust of a bayonet,
Reaching a blossom in rust of shrapnel.

JOURNALIST

After the Spanish-American War, Carl tried to figure out what to do with his life. While he worked as a fireman in Galesburg, he thought about becoming a journalist, a poet, an actor—even a congressman. Because he had left school after eighth grade to help his family, he was hungry for the education he had missed. In 1898 Carl took classes at Lombard College in Galesburg. The next year he was nominated by his congressman and the officers of Company C to enroll at West Point—if he could pass the entrance examinations. He failed the mathematics and grammar tests, but Carl didn't give up. He returned to Lombard, where he again took classes, edited the yearbook, and wrote speeches and poems.

After college Carl moved to Chicago and earned his first paychecks as a journalist. He then moved to Milwaukee, Wisconsin, to write newspaper stories and to make speeches for the Social Democratic Party. He and other party members fought for equal rights, better schools, and higher pay for workers like Carl's father.

In 1907 Carl met Lilian Anna Maria Elizabeth Steichen, a schoolteacher. Lilian and Carl quickly discovered that they shared a love for poetry, politics—and each other. They married in 1908, and Carl soon began working full-time as a reporter. Could he be both a journalist and a poet? Lilian thought so. She encouraged him to keep writing poems, and she typed them neatly on their old typewriter.

Carl usually reported stories about politics, crime, and injustice, but in 1909 he wrote about Abraham Lincoln, his hero. In honor of Lincoln's one-hundredth birthday, the U.S. Treasury introduced a new copper penny with Lincoln's face on the coin. Carl wrote an article for the *Milwaukee Daily News* about why he thought this was a good idea.

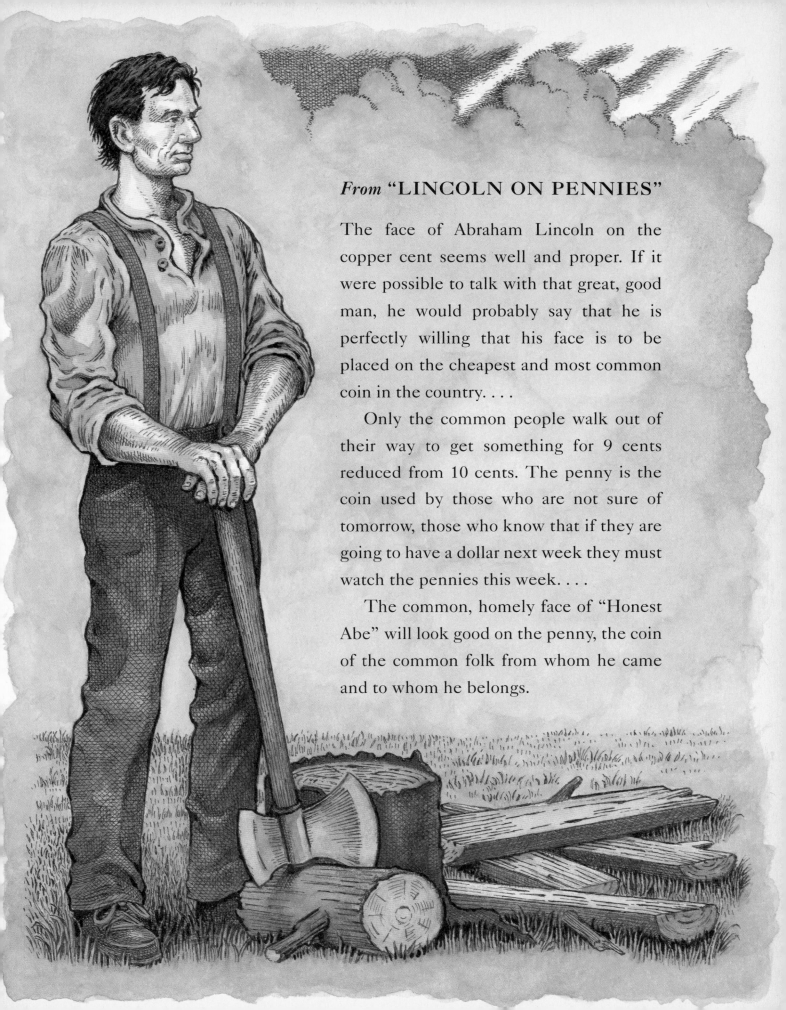

From "LINCOLN ON PENNIES"

The face of Abraham Lincoln on the copper cent seems well and proper. If it were possible to talk with that great, good man, he would probably say that he is perfectly willing that his face is to be placed on the cheapest and most common coin in the country. . . .

Only the common people walk out of their way to get something for 9 cents reduced from 10 cents. The penny is the coin used by those who are not sure of tomorrow, those who know that if they are going to have a dollar next week they must watch the pennies this week. . . .

The common, homely face of "Honest Abe" will look good on the penny, the coin of the common folk from whom he came and to whom he belongs.

MINSTREL

When Carl was a boy, he made his own musical instruments. He carved a willow whistle, covered a comb with paper to make a kazoo, and turned a cigar box into a banjo. Later he taught himself to strum a few simple chords on the guitar. He grew up to be a musician who loved to write poetry and a poet who loved to sing.

As Carl became famous for his writing, he traveled across the United States to speak about his books. Wherever he went, he collected folk songs. Many had never been written down, so when Carl heard people singing, he scribbled the words and tunes in his pocket notebooks. He learned songs about cornfields, prisons, and love. At home or in auditoriums where he spoke, Carl pulled out his guitar and sang some of his favorites: "She'll Be Comin' Round the Mountain," "The Foggy, Foggy Dew," or "Hallelujah, I'm a Bum!"

In 1926, long before audiotapes, CDs, and DVDs were invented, Carl recorded songs for the RCA Victor Talking Machine Company. Over the years he made more than two dozen records of songs, poems, and stories. In 1927 Carl gathered 280 folk songs in *The American Songbag*, a book of music about pioneers, pretty girls, soldiers, railroad workers, lumberjacks—even horses and frogs.

Carl loved folk and classical music, but he didn't approve of rock and roll (although he *did* like Elvis Presley). He listened to jazz, and heard so many musicians play in Chicago that he captured their finger-snapping, foot-tapping rhythms in some of his poems.

From JAZZ FANTASIA

Drum on your drums, batter your banjoes,
sob on the long cool winding saxaphones.
Go to it, O jazzmen.

Sling your knuckles on the bottoms of the happy
tin pans, let your trombones ooze, and go husha-
husha-hush with the slippery sand-paper.

Moan like an autumn wind high in the lonesome
treetops, moan soft like you wanted somebody
terrible, cry like a racing car slipping away from a
motorcycle cop, bang-bang! you jazzmen, bang
altogether drums, traps, banjoes, horns, tin cans . . .

FAMILY MAN

By 1918 Carl and Lilian had three daughters—Margaret, Janet, and Helga. Carl called his family the homeyglomeys, and gave the girls nicknames: "Spink" for Margaret, "Skabootch" for Janet, and "Swipes" for Helga. Spink was a bookworm, Skabootch was a homebody, and Swipes was a tomboy.

The Sandburgs lived in Illinois from 1912 until 1928, when they built a house on the Lake Michigan dunes near Harbert, Michigan. The whole family liked to swim in the lake, and Swipes rode her horse on the beach. She loved animals, large and small, and made up her mind that she wanted a cow. Her parents talked her into getting a goat instead, and soon Swipes and her mother began to raise goats.

In 1945 the Sandburgs moved to Connemara, a beautiful farm in Flat Rock, North Carolina. Built before the Civil War, the house is surrounded by mountains, woods, and meadows. At Connemara, with more pastureland, the Sandburgs owned hundreds of goats. Each kid was bottle-fed and given a special name, such as Bluebell, Cloverleaf Carlotta, and Dewrose.

Wherever they lived, the Sandburgs spent time together; they took long walks, often singing on their way. Carl collected "keepsakes" from nature—buckeyes, stones, and leaves that caught his eye. He stored them on bookshelves or in cigar boxes. In his writing room, he surrounded himself with a jumble of those keepsakes, along with papers, books, and magazines. At the dinner table, Carl often read his poems or stories aloud to the family. He taught his daughters to use their imaginations, and to love and respect nature, music—and words.

LITTLE GIRL, BE CAREFUL
WHAT YOU SAY

Little girl, be careful what you say
when you make talk with words, words—
for words are made of syllables
and syllables, child, are made of air—
and air is so thin—air is the breath of God—
air is finer than fire or mist,
finer than water or moonlight,
finer than spider-webs in the moon,
finer than water-flowers in the morning:
     and words are strong, too,
       stronger than rocks or steel
stronger than potatoes, corn, fish, cattle,
and soft, too, soft as little pigeon-eggs,
soft as the music of hummingbird wings.
     So, little girl, when you speak greetings,
when you tell jokes, make wishes or prayers,
     be careful, be careless, be careful,
     be what you wish to be.

STORYTELLER

Carl knew how to tell stories because he knew how to *listen* to them. He liked to hear people talk about their lives, and he collected their jokes and tall tales. In his travels and in books, he discovered the adventures and triumphs of everyday people. His poems often told stories, and he invented fairy tales for Spink, Skabootch, and Swipes. He wanted to make them laugh, and to comfort Spink, who was sick for a long time.

In 1922 Carl's fairy tales were published in a book called *Rootabaga Stories*. A rutabaga is a big, lumpy yellow turnip. When he was a boy in Galesburg, Carl ate rutabagas, and each fall, at the county fair, he saw the blue-ribbon rutabaga—the biggest one grown for miles around. He changed the spelling of *rutabaga* to *rootabaga* when he created Rootabaga Country, the magic land where his stories take place.

Carl wanted to give his children American fairy tales, not just stories about princes and princesses from Europe. Instead of hearing about Snow White, Prince Charming, or Cinderella, the Sandburg sisters listened as their father invented American characters named Blixie Blimber, Henry Hagglyhoagly, and Jason Squiff, who wears popcorn mittens and popcorn shoes.

In Rootabaga Country, people travel on the Zigzag Railroad to the Village of Liver-and-Onions, the Village of Cream Puffs, and a place called Medicine Hat, near the Saskatchewan River. Pigs wear bibs and rag dolls marry broom handles. In the farm fields, thousands of corn fairies dressed in overalls work hard to help the corn grow.

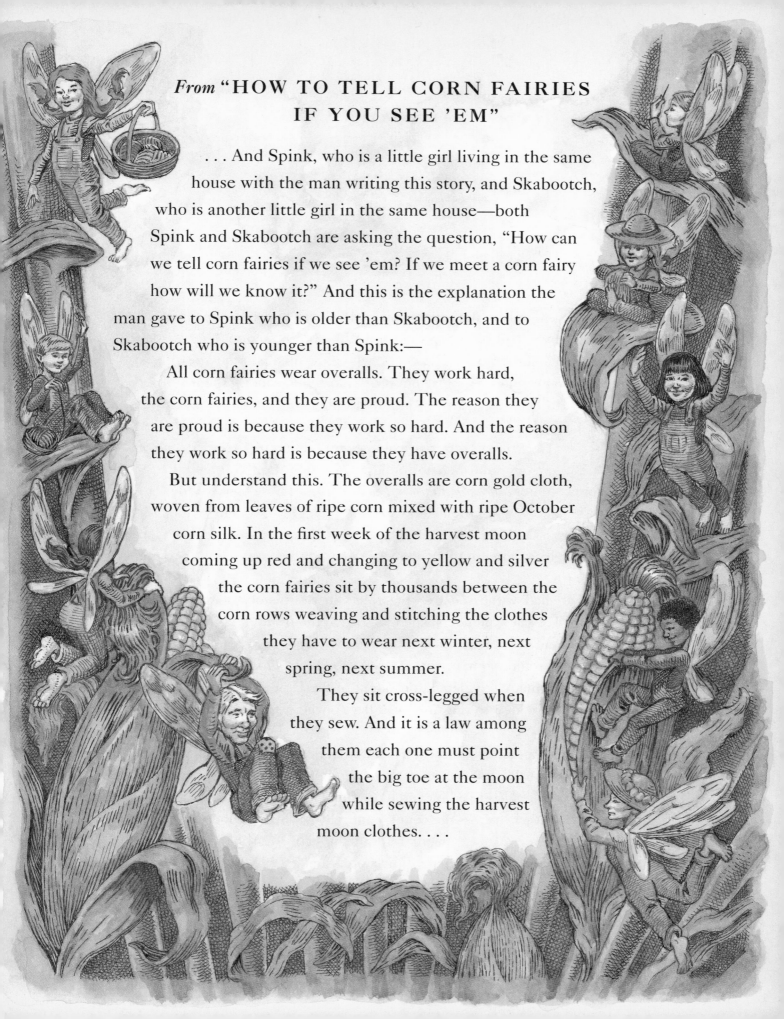

From "HOW TO TELL CORN FAIRIES IF YOU SEE 'EM"

. . . And Spink, who is a little girl living in the same house with the man writing this story, and Skabootch, who is another little girl in the same house—both Spink and Skabootch are asking the question, "How can we tell corn fairies if we see 'em? If we meet a corn fairy how will we know it?" And this is the explanation the man gave to Spink who is older than Skabootch, and to Skabootch who is younger than Spink:—

All corn fairies wear overalls. They work hard, the corn fairies, and they are proud. The reason they are proud is because they work so hard. And the reason they work so hard is because they have overalls.

But understand this. The overalls are corn gold cloth, woven from leaves of ripe corn mixed with ripe October corn silk. In the first week of the harvest moon coming up red and changing to yellow and silver the corn fairies sit by thousands between the corn rows weaving and stitching the clothes they have to wear next winter, next spring, next summer.

They sit cross-legged when they sew. And it is a law among them each one must point the big toe at the moon while sewing the harvest moon clothes. . . .

HISTORIAN

When Carl was a shoeshine boy in 1893, he polished the boots of soldiers who had fought in the Civil War. He listened to their memories of his hero, Abraham Lincoln, who grew up a poor boy in Illinois and became famous for his honesty, wisdom, and courage. Thirty years later Carl decided to write a children's biography about Honest Abe.

That idea grew into seven books. In 1926 Carl finished *Abraham Lincoln: The Prairie Years*, two volumes for adults. In 1928 *Abe Lincoln Grows Up* was published for children. In 1939 Carl completed four more volumes, *Abraham Lincoln: The War Years*. Those books made Carl world famous, and in 1940 he won the Pulitzer Prize for History for *The War Years*. On February 12, 1959, Carl made a speech to a joint session of Congress, honoring President Lincoln on the 150th anniversary of his birth.

Carl had witnessed exciting times in the history of the United States. He knew pioneers who had settled the frontier. He had been a soldier and wartime journalist. He had seen laws change so that African Americans and women won the right to vote. During Carl's lifetime eighteen men were elected president of the United Sates and twelve stars were added to the American flag for the new states admitted to the union.

Carl appreciated electricity, automobiles, airplanes, telephones, radio, and television because he remembered the days before those inventions made life easier and more fun. He flew as an honored guest on the first jet to cross the country and saw newspaper photographs of the first American astronauts to orbit the earth. Carl believed in the future because he understood the storms and dreams of the past.

EVER A SEEKER

The fingers turn the pages.
The pages unfold as a scroll.
There was the time there was no America.
Then came on the scroll an early
   America, a land of beginnings,
   an American being born.
Then came a later America, seeker
   and finder, yet ever more seeker
   than finder, ever seeking its way
   amid storm and dream.

PEN PAL

Carl wrote hundreds of letters to friends and fans all over the world. When he was traveling, he wrote love letters to Lilian and cheerful notes to his children. He received so much mail that bundles of letters were delivered to Connemara in baskets. He wrote in code on each letter. *Blah* meant he would not answer that letter. *AA* meant "Answer Anytime," but he never got around to answering those letters. *F* meant "Fellowship," and he would answer those letters as soon as he could.

Carl wrote nearly thirty short, friendly paragraphs that his secretary could use to answer mail from strangers. He called those paragraphs his form letters and gave each one a number. He marked a code number on every letter, so that the secretary would know how to answer. For example, people who asked for advice got answer 12: "My only advice to you is to beware of advice and to be never afraid of toil, solitude and prayer." Answer 25 said: "May great constellations and bright luck stars hover over you all your born days."

Carl exchanged letters with famous people, including Helen Keller, Elvis Presley, Robert Frost, Ernest Hemingway, and King Gustav of Sweden, who awarded him the Litteris et Artibus medal in 1959 for being a great Swedish-American writer. He wrote letters to Presidents Franklin D. Roosevelt, Harry S. Truman, John F. Kennedy, and Lyndon B. Johnson. Carl wrote to President Truman on September 15, 1945, after the president thanked him for the gift of the Lincoln biographies.

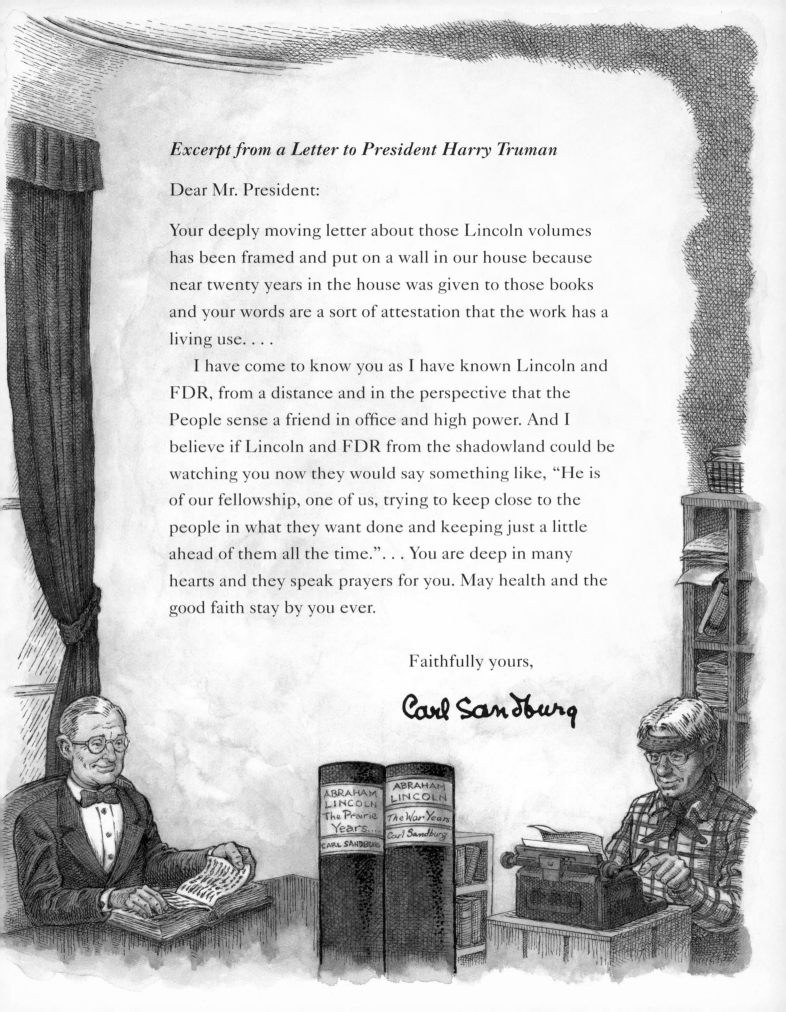

Excerpt from a Letter to President Harry Truman

Dear Mr. President:

Your deeply moving letter about those Lincoln volumes has been framed and put on a wall in our house because near twenty years in the house was given to those books and your words are a sort of attestation that the work has a living use. . . .

I have come to know you as I have known Lincoln and FDR, from a distance and in the perspective that the People sense a friend in office and high power. And I believe if Lincoln and FDR from the shadowland could be watching you now they would say something like, "He is of our fellowship, one of us, trying to keep close to the people in what they want done and keeping just a little ahead of them all the time.". . . You are deep in many hearts and they speak prayers for you. May health and the good faith stay by you ever.

Faithfully yours,

Carl Sandburg

DREAMER

Carl called himself a seeker and a dreamer. As a boy who lived surrounded by the prairie, he had dreamed about seeing the ocean. He imagined standing onshore, watching a ship sail out to sea until the round earth hid its sails from view. He also imagined sailing on the ship, watching the land fade away.

Carl daydreamed about stories he read. He could picture Paul Revere galloping through the night to warn that the British were coming, and George Washington leading ragged soldiers into battle. He read a popular children's book, *Toby Tyler: or, Ten Weeks with a Circus*, and wished that he could share Toby's circus adventures.

Like so many American boys then and now, Carl dreamed about playing major-league baseball. When he was sixteen, he ran to catch a fly ball and gashed his right foot on a broken bottle. He got four stitches and gave up his hope of becoming a baseball player. But he kept dreaming about other worlds he would explore, adventures he would have, and books he would write, believing "Nothing happens unless first a dream."

Carl wrote many words about the American Dream of equal rights and opportunity. He dreamed of a time when people around the globe would live in peace, not in fear of nuclear war. He believed children could grow up to take good care of the earth, and make a safer, happier world. Carl wrote about the mysteries of life and the wonders of nature—storms and stars, and sunsets that dance across the skies before dusk and dreamtime.

SUNSETS

There are sunsets who whisper a good-by.
It is a short dusk and a way for stars.
Prairie and sea rim they go level and even
And the sleep is easy.

There are sunsets who dance good-by.
They fling scarves half to the arc,
To the arc then and over the arc.
Ribbons at the ears, sashes at the hips,
Dancing, dancing good-by. And here sleep
Tosses a little with dreams.

POET

Carl found inspiration for poems on streetcars and trains, along main streets and harbor docks, in skyscrapers and steel mills, and under midnight stars. He remembered the beauty of the prairie roads he had walked as a boy, the plowed fields stretching to the horizon, the people working hard from sunrise to sunset. He put those memories in poems, along with his love for his family and his country.

Carl wrote while riding on trains, working in cluttered offices, or sitting under evergreen trees on the rocky slope behind his house in North Carolina. First he scribbled ideas in pencil, then pecked out the poems with two fingers on an old typewriter. He wrote about hard times and high hopes. He poured the experiences of real life into his poetry. People read and remembered his poems because they felt Carl was speaking to them. They believed that he understood and cared about their struggles and joys.

In 1951 Carl won the Pulitzer Prize for Poetry for *Complete Poems*. By then he was one of the most famous writers in the world. Carl called his face his *phizzog*, a slang word for *physiognomy*, meaning "face." Because so many people read his poems and heard him speak, his "phizzog" was featured on magazine covers, in newspapers, and on television.

Carl Sandburg died at Connemara on July 22, 1967. He was eighty-nine. Thousands of people gathered at the Lincoln Memorial in Washington, D.C., the following September to celebrate his life and work. His ashes are buried in Galesburg, in the garden of the house by the railroad tracks where he watched the trains go by and dreamed of faraway places.

PLOWBOY

After the last red sunset glimmer,
Black on the line of a low hill rise,
Formed into moving shadows, I saw
A plowboy and two horses lined against the gray,
Plowing in the dusk the last furrow.
The turf had a gleam of brown,
And smell of soil was in the air,
And, cool and moist, a haze of April.

I shall remember you long,
Plowboy and horses against the sky in shadow.
I shall remember you and the picture
You made for me,
Turning the turf in the dusk
And haze of an April gloaming.

TIME LINE 1865–1968

For eighty-nine years, Carl Sandburg lived through hard times and happy times—war as well as peace, poverty as well as wealth. Like his friends and neighbors, he saw great changes take place in the United States and around the world. He watched and listened carefully, and wrote about what angered or inspired him, and what he wanted to celebrate.

When Carl was a boy, the train was the fastest, best way to travel. By the time he was an adult, there were automobiles and airplanes—and later, even rockets to the moon. As a boy, in the days before electricity, Carl read books at night by the light of an oil lamp. As a grown man, he could often be heard on radio programs and seen on television.

Just as one person can help change the world, world events can change individual lives. All that Carl witnessed and lived through helped shape the man he was—and the writer he became. This time line traces some of the moments, large and small, that were important in Carl Sandburg's lifetime and in his work.

CARL SANDBURG'S LIFE

1869 Father August Sandburg emigrates from Sweden to the United States

1873 Mother Clara Anderson emigrates from Sweden to the United States

1878 Carl August Sandburg born, January 6, in Galesburg, Illinois

1891 Confirmed at Elim Lutheran Church; leaves school to earn money for family

1894 First train trip, to Peoria for the Illinois State Fair

1896 First trip to Chicago

1897 Leaves Illinois for the first time; heads west as a vagabond looking for adventure and work

1898 Serves in the Spanish-American War

1902 First published poem, "The Falling Leaves," appears in *The Thistle*, a literary magazine

1905 Buys first typewriter

1906 Leaves Galesburg to work in Chicago

1908 Marries Lilian Anna Maria Elizabeth Steichen in Milwaukee, Wisconsin

1916 *Chicago Poems* published

1917 Travels to Sweden as a correspondent covering World War I

1919 *The Chicago Race Riots* published by Harcourt, Brace and Howe

1922 *Rootabaga Stories* published

1926 Records first album of songs for the RCA Victor Talking Machine Company; *Abraham Lincoln: The Prairie Years* published

1927 *The American Songbag* published

1928 *Abe Lincoln Grows Up* published

1936 *The People, Yes* published

1939 *Abraham Lincoln: The War Years* published

1940 Wins Pulitzer Prize for History, for *Abraham Lincoln: The War Years*

1945 Moves with his family to Connemara, a farm in Flat Rock, North Carolina

1946 Birthplace at Galesburg dedicated as historic site

1950 *Complete Poems* published

1951 Wins Pulitzer Prize for Poetry, for *Complete Poems*

1956 First of many U.S. schools named after him opens in Harvey, Illinois

1959 Delivers Lincoln Day Address before joint session of Congress;

1965 Honored by the National Association for the Advancement of Colored People (NAACP)

1967 Dies at Connemara, July 22; eulogized on September 17 at the Lincoln Memorial

1865 – 1874
1875 – 1884
1885 – 1894
1895 – 1904
1905 – 1914
1915 – 1924
1925 – 1934
1935 – 1944
1945 – 1954
1955 – 1964
1965 – 1968

HISTORIC EVENTS

1865 Civil War ends; President Abraham Lincoln assassinated in Washington, D.C.

1868 Typewriter patented

1869 Cincinnati (Ohio) Red Stockings founded as first professional baseball team

1882 Electric lighting introduced in New York City

1886 Statue of Liberty dedicated, gift to the United States from France

1889 North Dakota, South Dakota, Montana, and Washington become the 39th through 42d states

1890 Idaho and Wyoming become the 43d and 44th states

1896 Utah becomes the 45th state; first modern Olympic Games held in Athens, Greece

1898 Spanish-American War begins and ends

1903 First flight of Wilbur and Orville Wright, near Kitty Hawk, North Carolina; Ford Motor Company founded in Detroit, Michigan

1907 Oklahoma becomes the 46th state

1909 National Association for the Advancement of Colored People (NAACP) founded

1912 New Mexico and Arizona become the 47th and 48th states; SS *Titanic* sinks in the North Atlantic

1914 World War I begins (1914–18)

1917 First Pulitzer Prizes awarded

1920 19th amendment to the Constitution grants women the right to vote

1927 First commercial "talkie" film, *The Jazz Singer*, shown in theaters

1928 Cartoonist Walt Disney introduces Mickey Mouse character; bubble gum first sold

1929 Stock market crashes, sending United States into the Great Depression

1939 World War II begins (1939–45)

1950 Korean War begins (1950–53)

1954 U.S. Supreme Court outlaws "separate but equal" school segregation

1959 Alaska and Hawaii become the 49th and 50th states

1961 First American sent into space

1963 President John F. Kennedy assassinated in Dallas, Texas

1964 Martin Luther King Jr. receives Nobel Peace Prize

1965 Vietnam War begins (1965–75)

1968 Martin Luther King Jr. assassinated in Memphis, Tennessee; U.S. Senator and presidential candidate Robert F. Kennedy assassinated in Los Angeles, California

ILLUSTRATION NOTES

Marc Nadel's watercolor-and-crosshatch illustrations present historically accurate portraits of the diverse worlds in which Carl Sandburg lived. The images have been thoroughly researched, using family and archival photographs for reference for everything from the Chicago scene on the title spread to the Gettysburg battlefield for "New Feet" to the farm equipment in the artwork for "Plowboy."

Sandburg's personal possessions are featured in the illustrations. The museum at the Carl Sandburg Home National Historic Site—at Connemara, his final home, in Flat Rock, North Carolina—was generously opened to Nadel, who used the opportunity to photograph and sketch everything from Sandburg's shoes, awards, and pocketknife to the meadows, barnyards, and buildings on the farm. The notes that follow provide some biographical context for select illustrations.

JACKET: The back of the jacket presents a message in Carl's handwriting that first appeared on the cover of *Wind Song*, a collection of poems for children published in 1960.

TITLE SPREAD: Carl is walking past a typical warehouse building in Chicago, near the Lake Michigan harbor. Nadel's mural on the building is filled with objects that represent various periods of Carl's life and many of his accomplishments: the type of train that passed through Galesburg, Illinois, when he was young; milk bottles like those he carried as a "milk slinger"; his soldier's hat and medal from the Spanish-American War; his guitar; a copy of *Rootabaga Stories*, his first children's book; and a handwritten copy of the poem "Fog."

A WORLD OF WORDS: The house in the upper left corner is the home in Galesburg, Illinois, where Carl was born in 1878; the building in the bottom right corner is the main house at Connemara, the farm in Flat Rock, North Carolina, where he lived from 1945 until his death in 1967.

VAGABOND: The pocket watch, kerchief, pocketknife, and small notebook used for jotting down thoughts for newspaper articles and poems all belonged to Carl, who is shown riding in a boxcar.

SOLDIER: Carl was awarded this medal for serving in the U.S. Army in Puerto Rico during the Spanish-American War in 1898.

JOURNALIST: The glasses and the green visor belonged to Carl; he usually wore them when he worked because of his poor eyesight and sensitivity to light.

MINSTREL: Carl owned many guitars and taught himself to play. He used this guitar when he sang his favorite songs from *The American Songbag*, a collection of nearly three hundred songs, published in 1927, including the music and lyrics he gathered during his early travels throughout the United States. He dedicated the book "To those unknown singers—who made songs—out of love, fun, grief—and to those many other singers—who kept those songs as living things of the heart and mind."

FAMILY MAN: The gingko leaves, buckeyes, cigar box, and fountain pen can be seen today in the rooms at Connemara. The barn on the facing page was home to the goats raised by Carl's wife, Lilian, and their daughters Helga and Janet. (Offspring of the Sandburgs' goats still live on the farm.) The little girl is Carl's only granddaughter, Paula.

STORYTELLER: Carl appears as one of the corn fairies, swinging from a corn husk.

PEN PAL: Carl is shown in the lower right corner, pecking away on an old typewriter in his attic office and using an orange crate for a desk.

The illustrations were created on Strathmore Bristol 3-ply vellum using Kolinsky sable brushes with Winsor & Newton Watercolours; crosshatching was completed using Hunt hawk and crow quills, with Higgins waterproof drawing black India and brown inks.

ACKNOWLEDGMENTS

We thank the people whose ideas, encouragement, and support helped make this book possible: First, Anna Marlis Burgard of Harcourt, for her remarkable dedication, perception, and creativity, which imbue each page with intelligence and warmth; our own "Homeyglomeys": Jennifer Niven McJunkin, John Michael Hreno III, Lynn Niven Clark, Doris Niven Knapp, Bill Niven, and Nathaniel von Sprecken and Learyn von Sprecken, who helped their aunt Penny by reading parts of the manuscript; Nancy Shrewsbury Nadel, James Nadel, Bertha Nadel, and Mallie Nadel, for their enthusiasm, clever suggestions, and humor. Special appreciation goes out to Doris Knapp's fifth-grade class at North Elementary School in Lancaster, South Carolina, for reading a manuscript draft.

We send our gratitude to "Swipes," Carl Sandburg's daughter Helga, for her enduring inspiration and creative energy; to his granddaughter, Paula Steichen Polega, for her ideas, affirmation, and a wonderful picnic on a sunny March day in Flat Rock, North Carolina; to Maurice Greenbaum of the Carl Sandburg Family Trust, for facilitating permissions grants; to Connie Backlund and Warren Weber of Connemara, the Carl Sandburg Home National Historic Site in Flat Rock, for generously making treasures and resources (and even goats) available to us; to Lynn Savage, Staci Cummins, and Bess Gibbs, for their guidance in the Connemara museum and archives; to other members of the National Park Service staff, for sharing their expertise; to Carol Nelson and Steve Holden at the Carl Sandburg Birthplace in Galesburg, Illinois, for valuable assistance; and to members of the staff of the Fletcher Free Library in Burlington, Vermont, for their help and interest in this project.

We are grateful to the talented people at Harcourt who converted our words and images into the reality of this book: Robin Cruise, Ivan Holmes, and Pascha Gerlinger.

Finally, we thank Carl Sandburg, who lived this life. He has been for us, as he said Abraham Lincoln was for him, such good company.

—P. E. N. and M. D. N.

PERMISSIONS ACKNOWLEDGMENTS

"Fog" and "Plowboy" from *Chicago Poems* by Carl Sandburg, copyright © 1916 by Holt, Rinehart and Winston and renewed 1944 by Carl Sandburg; reprinted by permission of Harcourt, Inc.

"Just Before April Came" and "Jazz Fantasia" from *Smoke and Steel* by Carl Sandburg, copyright © 1920 by Harcourt, Inc. and renewed 1948 by Carl Sandburg; reprinted by permission of Harcourt, Inc.

"Baby Song of the Four Winds" and "Sunsets" from *Good Morning, America,* copyright © 1928 and renewed 1956 by Carl Sandburg; reprinted by permission of Harcourt, Inc.

"New Feet" from *Cornhuskers* by Carl Sandburg, copyright © 1918 by Holt, Rinehart and Winston and renewed 1946 by Carl Sandburg; reprinted by permission of Harcourt, Inc.

Excerpt from the article "Lincoln on Pennies" by Carl Sandburg first appeared in the *Milwaukee Daily News* on August 3, 1909

"Little Girl, Be Careful What You Say" from *The Complete Poems of Carl Sandburg,* copyright © 1970, 1969 by Lilian Steichen Sandburg, Trustee; reprinted by permission of Harcourt, Inc.

Excerpt from "How to Tell Corn Fairies If You See 'Em" from *Rootabaga Stories* by Carl Sandburg, copyright © 1923, 1922 by Harcourt, Inc. and renewed 1951, 1950 by Carl Sandburg; reprinted by permission of Harcourt, Inc.

"Ever a Seeker" from *The People, Yes* by Carl Sandburg, copyright © 1936 by Harcourt, Inc. and renewed 1964 by Carl Sandburg; reprinted by permission of Harcourt, Inc.

Excerpt from a letter to Harry S Truman in *The Letters of Carl Sandburg,* copyright © 1968 by Lilian Steichen Sandburg, Trustee; reprinted by permission of Harcourt, Inc.

Library of Congress Cataloging-in-Publication Data
Niven, Penelope.
Carl Sandburg: adventures of a poet/Penelope Niven; with poems and prose by Carl Sandburg; illustrated by Marc Nadel.
p. cm.
Summary: Traces the life of the American poet, journalist, and historian who won the Pulitzer Prize for Poetry and the Pulitzer Prize for History.
1. Sandburg, Carl, 1878–1967—Juvenile literature. 2. Poets, American—20th century—Biography—Juvenile literature.
[1. Sandburg, Carl, 1878–1967. 2. Poets, American.]
I. Sandburg, Carl, 1878–1967. II. Nadel, Marc, ill. III. Title.
PS3537.A618Z787 2003
811'.52—dc21 2002014592
ISBN 0-15-204686-0

H G F E D C B

The display type was set in Honduras.
The text type was set in Caslon.
Color separations by Bright Arts Ltd., Hong Kong
Printed in Singapore
Production supervision by Sandra Grebenar and Pascha Gerlinger
Designed by Ivan Holmes